In Ways
Impossible
to Fold

In Ways Impossible to Fold

Michael Rerick

EAST ROCKAWAY
MARSH HAWK PRESS • 2009

09 10 11 12 7 6 5 4 3 2 1 FIRST EDITION

Marsh Hawk Press books are published by Poetry Mailing List, Inc.,
a not-for-profit corporation under section 501 (c) 3 United States
Internal Revenue Code.

Cover art by Shaun Tan © 1996, 80 x 80 cm. Used by permission of the
artist. The title is "Norseman" (a very small, remote country town in
Western Australia). The materials are found objects from the actual
scene: machine parts, rusted tin cans, plaster, oils, beeswax and red
dust. The landscape image painted on the flat, nailed cans represents
the place where the objects and dust come from, near a huge flat salt
lake, Lake Cowan, dry all year except winter.

Book and cover design by Claudia Carlson
Author photograph by Kristi Maxwell

The text and display are set in Palatino

Library of Congress Cataloging-in-Publication Data

Rerick, Michael.
In ways impossible to fold / Michael Rerick. — 1st ed.
    p. cm.
ISBN-13: 978-0-9792416-8-0 (pbk.)
ISBN-10: 0-9792416-8-5 (pbk.)
I. Title.
PS3618.E78I6 2009
811'.6—dc22

                          2008037730

Marsh Hawk Press
P.O. Box 206, East Rockaway, N.Y. 11518-0206
www.marshhawkpress.org

Table of Contents

Acknowledgements

"Objects, a History" appears in *42opus* 4/9/08.

"(invisible wood and plastic form #1)" and "(grammatical projections)" appear in *Bathhouse* 4:1.

"(milk form sculpture)," (plane sculpture)," and "(lawn tower sculpture)" appear in *Coconut* 5.

"8" and "10" appear in *Court Green* 4.

"Post Clips" is forthcoming in *Drunken Boat*.

"1" won 3rd place in the 2005 SLS St. Petersburg/*Fence* poetry contest and appears in *Fence* 16.

"(at the tiny circus)" and "(exhibit T.M.)" appear in *Forklift, Ohio* Issue 17.

"(last call sculpture)" and "(form #7 in grass sculpture)" are forthcoming in *Greatcoat* 2.

"(invisible organ)," "(the technician)," and "9" appear in *Melancholia's Tremulous Dreadlocks* 7.

"6," "7," and "11" appear in *MIPOesias*, 8/20/06.

"(metal work)" and "(chess players)" appear in *Shampoo* 25.

"2," "3," "5," and "(public square)" appear in *Words on Walls* Issue 7.

"(exhibit 33)" was printed as a broadside for the Cy Press/Publico reading series.

"X-Ray" appears in the chapbook *X-Ray* out with Flying Guillotine Press.

Unconditional love and appreciation goes out to all the following made this book possible: Sandy McIntosh and everyone at Marsh Hawk Press, Thylias Moss, Thomas Fink, all my family, Tenney Nathanson, Boyer Rickel, Jane Miller, Jon Anderson, Steve Orlen, Barbara Cully and all in the her workshop, Melissa Koosmann, Dawn Pendergast, Tony Mancus, Sommer Browning, all my peers at UA, Mark Grote, Amy Fine and Nessie, the computer, and every supportive and inspiring person that I've absently left out.

For Kristi

.... *Sculptures*

(metal work)

This, publicly, takes a love story and unfolds geometrically
in ways impossible to fold. All around: a park. Inside:
hollow. The welts show, the granite pedestal moans a bird,
it jumps. At night it sings. The story of "what draws me to it,
personally" grows in the socket of a mossy eye, a field
of I-beams that float, pivot, tap, meow, or triangulate
the gravity of healthy problems. Rust meets another wind.
Light: a shiver and smile of wire mesh.

(at the tiny circus)

Lions thin as coat hangers pace beneath the trapeze
the way a flame flicks but caught between flicks.
The green, curly haired clown broods before catching
a pie, philosophical as a yo-yo. In each circle, twisted
wire joints bob. Rice eyes on marionette command,
steel thread ending at air. Ring master. Ring master.
Ring master. Implied tent, stakes dizzy in the wind.
The wood horse clops to the sound of peanut shells.

(milk form)

Caught falling from the glass or pouring
from the body: white. Fluid plastic—
appendage in cast. Or the glass alone.
A beaker filled lab, test-tubes of cream,
oscillate and hum, meringue whip sealed
in camouflaged boxes. To one side:
a bucket to catch, a cold hand on the teat.

(plane)

Sticks arc-smooth:
an egg from the
naked revisited
human body, and
some knee, some
hair, some nipple
some rib, some
part treated
wood: time
machine snuck in
the center: air as
cloud cover: sea
as sandy: it floats
three stories.

(chess players)

The sixty-four square 0 point, hub, radii,
disappears. Or, arc follows players. Non-
violent field: sweat and ambush: froze.
One calls, one responds in this equation-church.
Disengaged or pensive: rook in advance, retreat,
advance. The queen starts on her own color,
before mate and after. Fingers reach for the king
from many positions.

(public square)

Rough tiles hold building toss in water
and water ripple. Polished metal sprouts mirrors
in a slow spiral, one level, air, one level, air, one level
air, between steps, air. Light cloaks what avenue
convergence undoes. Soapstone.

(last call)

Figures circle like most circles (wedding, funeral, dance, barricade) around a thing obstructed. All water ripple skinned or smooth and dark cherry lacquered lean out, all but one primed aqua. The one in leans but shouts the rest out: none have a face to drink, eat, or breathe but keep the circle and point center. Their iron feet match the floor, they are height high, they are thin.

(form # 7 in grass)

Metal wraps a silver blanket around a motor cooling from the heat of work: rusting in the sun. Tall blades cut along the shore of the lake. This ship, moored for the freight of seeing: rust, polished steel, a little blue paint. Coordinates, slope, and angles, all angled and sloped, too uneven to sit on or stand by—the metal plows and the weather slips all around and off. Most corners are pockets difficult to breathe in, and it rises as a radar tower.

(exhibition T. M.)

A living room sized stapler of paper.
A promise, in chocolate, carried by bees.
Leg of discarded cigarette butts, end to end.
Jar of pennies in process of spilling.
Self-portrait, as multiple overripe figures in a pool hall.
"Look behind you." Behind: "Look behind you."
Declaration of Independence writ in Christmas lights.
A smoke cloud suspended on a pedestal.
A fragment of sun of rain, mixed media.
Displayed ant brain behind 3" stainless steel.

(invisible organ)

Cast in silicate gas slick, raised, delicate—
how she looks in blue, he's entering in red.
Particular chambers, if chambers or surface
or spectra and observers, bend and blur away.
Up to the lights, works color on the walls.

(grammatical projections)

The hottest part of wire makes: light. Wire: light. A slick bed of fiber optic, red, under plastic. Make letters. Flicks repeat, beds and beds of neon. Reading a way from under water, too, onto the white wall, to read. The off parts: cavities, but in context of hot extension cords. Spelled: tangent across the large cityscape but smaller from a distance: it's not the message.

(lawn tower)

Stacked in dirt squares—
what supported feet:
bare on Christmas;
arms: rash, later
thought disease; eyes:
rain on blades
through rain—in
a square of electric.
It's water fed, because
soaked. Weeds grow:
stubbornly weeding
gloveless, his hands
bled; she remembers
the sun, now a wearer
of hats. Tiered
for stability
the fence hums.

(the technician)

A tanker pumps into the glass trap. Underwater
coils of wire and tubing bubble: an iron figure
cleans with whirring brush-feet and fizzing hose-
arms. Air behind the glass face-plate: a mirror: no
edge where the tank ends, no indication which
hose pushes water, which gas, where the air goes.
The monitor hangs, swings, repeats.

(invisible wood and plastic form #1)

Parts of parts miss, but portions of trees
of clouds of glass and marble align into:
a round. Planet glowing without hook
or wire. Like perfection in idea, an idea.
The circumference bends into an equation
children play on. Dust catches in the probability
of points sketched in coordinates of what
part the day occurs. Depending what year,
what color. Shades brighter when light slacks
into finer distinctions of what light is.

(exhibit 33)

Speakers play three hundred harps in the greenhouse.
Metal, rolled shutters open the milky glass to the hot air.
Worms, video projected, dance on yellow pansies
in a low box. Transmitted flies crawl over a live saguaro.
The harps play "Nothing Grows" to roaches of light
appearing and disappearing in the needles
of a Douglas fir. Misters bead the air blue between
animals and plants. The door, heavier than it looks,
pulls tight on its hinges. The first thing thought: harps.

.... *X-Ray*

In and over folds form and form it. At night, wet under
rags: as if I never touched it—
when fired, it is fire—
cut from the ground, it wants to be clay.
My hands, like butterflies in mud, let my fingers be furious.

Floating. A railroad spike through my
chest and into the mattress, but the
stomach, it floats. I see it rising, and
I'm with it, though my chest is sinking,
there is the stomach, floating.

From the sharpest heaps, the dullest parts:
2x4s split from nails,
metal rusted ghost,
green and pink plastics,
boiled and cooled fractured marbles,
twisted with concrete chicken wire,
tree limbs.
Drag them into the warm inside.
Then wax, reckless with wax:
coat and coat until it's a positive milk cloud.

The pain stills. One of her fingers
between two of mine, then another touch
and I am almost, completely, covered.

Thinking kitchen
                    the word comes out electric
smoke and I want to ladle you. Spilled milk
                    and green on the floor:
answers come in the form of a fridge, a freezer, a glass dance
  on a thin film of water.
I build a copy
over a ball-bearing floor: everything still, except the floor.

My forehead, cold. I pull the covers and am
distant from the covers. She puts her arm
over me. She puts her arm over my chest,
where it should hurt but does not.

Stone lasts too long, past
most heat. But certain days
        demand it. When dates float,
I remember

        at night I played her boob like a bagpipe,

before I found stone, before

        the chest

the ghost from stone,

        her breath cold on my back. Her breath
        makes me ill and I am ashamed.

I work and forget and remember.
The stone slightly undresses imperfect.

With her back to me I negotiate the breathablity of fabric, covers. Her body, her weight. She turns, injects my joints with just one of her legs.

                                        Fabric. Sag and
the cloth mother for the baby monkey.
                        How the adult monkey felt going out
in clothes, among other adults in clothes
                to parties where, having too much to drink,
the monkey cries
                on the soft shoulder pad of a stranger.

I unravel bolts of white shag and make rabbits.
Thousands of rabbits.
                        Am I Albert,
                        the man they trained
                        against

the accomplishment
                of all these rabbits at my feet?

Texture must be me
under a bush,
      scattered along a curb,
a shiny piece of skin half buried in the dirt.
          Found   things.
With other material
              spread across the floor, or stacks,
      or interlocks.
The material makes   itself.   Adhesives—
      glue, wax, concrete,
metal and flux—restricted to the way material sticks.

She says she sees in X-ray, through me.
I feel afraid of the side effects. She says
the problem is not lead, but dermises.

          Molding the air, I become less.
I wonder if people see,
or notice this half-person.
      The way air reworks
eye color, takes the top part of a mountain away, or addition:
      layers and layers of a new thing,
and with less transparency than would seem possible.

I stretch and miss the specks of light
floating in the room, the tunnel-vision.
My mind wanders. She says this is
when I see her clearest, which is true,
which scares me: I will eventually fall
wholly one way or the other.

Trained: knowing
        a thing behind the thing,
suggestions suggesting
        curiosity: how far seeing goes,
how pins suddenly
        proliferate and
come together. I want
        to loosen my house
and remake a found box.

She warns me away from heavy
sweaters and smoke. In the evening
the air is lighter. It's difficult to sleep.
Certain pressures gone.

Rubber bands.

                                         A window of them,
a guitar. Self-portrait:
grows brittle and crumbles.
                          No warnings
                                    elastic effects over the body.
The trick: subtract the funny noise novelty
to take out the utility of binding.

This is true of most things,
but most true of rubber bands.

            Because we refuse the hospital. She tells
            me her life is not the dream I think it is
            because some things we do not finish.

My cat's purr dies. Advised Wittgenstein and letters—acids
and bleach, stray cats striped down (how his hands ran with
chemical filled fur)—the preservation of my little dead. The
pose and placement in the house. Taxidermists bleed the idea.
Instead, I help her die, altogether.

            For months a teapot sloshes in my stomach.
            She feeds me mint turning my yellow skin
            green—the slow way my chest works, I
            breathe little puffs of steam—in the mirror
            a blurred train look.

A hard case through quick molds—
      water flow mixes with the body, makes the body: form.
Wax a hollow illusion of weight, bronze with the heavy trick
  of movement.
      Casts—rough, jagged—to be buffed: waxed metal.

        She puts a hat on my head when I'm in the
        shade but the sun moves.

The pliability trick of wood …its soak smell
bends to be discovered—rediscovered—
with a balance of time and portions…
experiments with temperature,
with humidity, and light… heat lamps vs. the sun…
the hardening… convincing.

        I say, you are to me a miracle of soft gears.
        She confesses she sees a small red ball
        rolling in her mouth.

Material smoothed to hide material
crammed with everything I know, cram more,
but only makes more and more room. The box project
will not finish. Its size and texture grow soft.
I drag it in and out of the corner, surprised
each time by the weight, how it never changes.
Also, how the corner grows larger.

Oiled sheet metal piles dribble
rusty grit, rough edges from
the clipper. My I-beams against
the wall. Archimedes tinkered
this to mechanical novelties
and concurred human labor. I
crane to make light.

I promise. She says, my usefulness, my
usefulness and takes parts away, or
they melt.

Instructions say   metal should look lighter than metal is
must tell the viewer
              the possibility of falling with weightlessness.
But I want to make a heavy thing look heavier.

She says, I know something famous
about you. This flatters me.

The small-town-of-metal project funds come slow. Every tree, every house and every carpet in every house, metal. Even dirt. Even air. Converging winds will make the town sing the hard song of appearing soft.
No inhabitant can know.

Every day I walk and speak in the hallucination. She says, I will not disappear. I say I will not disappear. We marry this idea.

When cracked and cooled how large and smooth the spinning planet cores. Caldrons hold metal and glass the same shape and glow.

.... *Objects, a History*

Swiss, great-grandmother says "blood" to the row of the river boat gently covering its tracks. Father defends their western terms, "I'm no wagon, no horse." Anchored—land, land ho—grandfather's in the motor, radio, hull, in the rain. Aunt J says "he touched it, it's ruined" and pops bread from a bread pan. Uncles talk Canada, a state away, with its good hunting, fishing.

Son-rock, father-rock, etc. Everyone has their own, and an everybody boulder. The married-in feel left out. Ambassadors dust pieces of quartz: "here." Moss gives them value.

The mother Northwest, "particle pants shirt other particles," shirt under coat in flannel. Daughter can only wool. The father underwears with holes. Son replicates grandmother in green and brown (a tree in a snow coat). All say, sweaters.

At the reunion picture sun hits all their eyes silver, a family of robots smiling off in different directions. Thanksgiving ends with the spoon game, eye glasses removed to prevent glass shards, glasses full of gin. Christmas surrounded by cold windows and the symmetry of grandma-grandpa, aunt-uncle, cousin-cousin.

Across country: a fast sit. Q: are cars unnatural shapes? Comfortable, the drive-in on gravel humps, to singing speakers. A: we make them. In some lifetime they will fly.

Aunt J and uncle B of the cats and dogs and chickens (raspberries, blueberries, grapes, broccoli, carrot, rhubarb—wheat bread, jam, ice cream... woodstove [girl scouts, babysitters]). Aunt J of the cats and dog (raspberries, grapes, broccoli, carrot, rhubarb—bread, jam... woodstove [girl scouts]).

No mention, we all do weird things in the bathroom. Kitchen dishes a certain melancholy in the mother. The grandfather digs, trails sharp coast shells. A family plot of cups for summer water fights. During holidays: juice and milk and whiskey.

The son hikes with grandmother in a lava field sharp but soft (exterior) from wind (everything exterior). Happy in wood in thicket in forest (a lightning starts). Uncle J deserts, cooks adobe, adobe home, like an oven. The son dreams old buildings of brick: supposed higher incidence of radiation (a microwave dings). When brother P drives: a suspicious parking job. Some particle board, some drywalls: plaster (a foot and fist temptation display).

When I die, the son says, throw me in a ditch. Father says religion "is a moon, then the long hike to a moon." Meanwhile, the mother clears floor space for strangers through the door. No grandparent keeps a family tree because the ridiculous shape.

Brother to the brother, I will tell the truth about music— because breakfast sounds like a railroad crossing—it is the whistle, the way air shakes. Brother tells the brother, I accept, and the truth of desirability: one more desirable than the other. Brother answers brother, a different tree color, a portrait, a house bent with old age. Brothers trade sides, tap feet, and listen to record grooves.

.... *Post Clips*

Dear Frank… here's the Du. *dwaal* altar cloth draped
like Christmas lights from a balcony—you always saw
tits—and a dark Czech beer at Sv. Norbert monastery…
dear Frank, she glows with the cold: the glass mug, 200 kč,
stenciled Sv. Norbert in gold, the body barrel and dimpled.

*

Seoul Tower, *n.* a tip and lights:
pandemic 360 of city, the absent river running through

knit, *n.* neon crosses blurred into very small, soft teeth

*

No dissolution in the marionette parting the curtain
and winks—the many folds from the little hand,
a peripheral detail. Transitions: the small body for home,
large for intricate dreamscapes, O.E. *bwean*, to wash
and fall in a thin aqua sea a pirate floats on. Prague children watch
with Prague parents and suck suckers at intermission.

*

0 floor:
our coats and scarves and hats
(ticket, ticket) and through
the hall of symphony faces

staircase:
dead leaders, The National Museum

1st floor:
rocks—outside we step on them—
in rows of normal/dazzle
(mineralogy + petrology = 200000 specimens)
while we see them, all fragments, all together

2nd floor:
Zoological
adj. bone (marrow)
n. boned:
platypus
fin whale (across the roof, the size of our apartment)
the giant: sea sponge (Poterion neptuni), Japanese crab, and clam

3rd floor:
city *n.* Kokoschka

*

Children (*cild*, Frank, *cild*) along the white morning
boardwalk, the concrete plaza.
The bay's too dirty to swim in,
gasoline angels (*angaros*: Oriental).
I'm up, leaving behind
coat and shoes and others.

Later, teenagers play soccer to mariachi
or corrido or Madonna.

*

We pick and cook around the grill, dip communally
with thin metal chopsticks the meat and vegetables in
sauces, use individual cloth *sugeons* for our lips and fingers.

*

Torture museum lithograph: a man spread feet-up,
two person saw half through him; reproduction:
pyramid to sit to death on. Water:
cloth tube in the throat filled and pulled out, filled, pulled out,
filled and pulled out
(Ger. *Zwagen*, verb first recorded 1836),
no phonemes left in the bruises.

*

I faked those moments in the books and radio.
A real Klimt is paint and beautiful.
6 violins, 2 cellos, 1 bass and 1 harpsichord do make Four Seasons.
I'm seeing a figure turned church by Bill Viola.

*

A wall—*toile, tulle, tavola, towel*—of recurrent "…wash my hands of… "

*

Collocations:
We mirror-maze with picture flashes;
Prague Castle/Petřin Hill, two ideas
on the same landmass, one imposing,
the other ice to the maze,
communal strangers laughing at strangers slipping
or reflecting in bent glass graffitied: glass-towel,
1, to wipe away, 2, to stiffen.

*

Egg *(oyyo)* and hamburger (Ger. immigrants 1939) and rice
  (vrihi-s-oryza)
under brown gravy *(ah ah)* at the drive-in, loco-moco especial,
weeks before Kilauea makes no-locals and a black ember-field. Legends
of the old goddess being *eggja* O.N.; and the rough waves
at the black sand beach wiped away.

*

trans. v. To apply... *he didn't know to [...] himself*

intr. v. (with at)... *he began* toweling *at his hands with the warm baby-wipe*

towel, *n.* food instrument; paper, with at least two equal sides; usage:
for what food will do; *his* towel *could not wipe up the stains*

*

Gyeongbokgung Palace houses the Sujeongjeon building
  (first script):
reconstruction from burnings, the plaque reads indecipherable
what a rock looks like on fire. I undo my scarf and slide the plastic
accordion curtain to the toilet. It's heated. Later, I take a picture of
  a stove
for water for the queen and forget what it's called.

*

As you can see the buildings are old,
and sanitary conditions—Lat. *sānitās*—
require thorough alcohol scrubbings.
Or the buildings are new:
we're getting clean clean clean.
We'll bring a big bottle of it back.

*

Hotel? *Quoi?* In too late for a sit down
meal, an arcade of fast food. *Jeter la*
serviette. We're nervous to the
street kid leading "Oh Canada!" to the
liquor store: not a materialization. Hungry,
so grab the first bed, *j'ai sommeil*, and sleep.

*

Seoul Land, *n.*, an amusement park in Seoul, Korea
sanitary belt, *n.*, a belt for the attachment of a sanitary towel
photograph, *n.*, *v.*,

*

Dongdaemun Market high-rise/stalls makes a 24 hour city of
  crowd—
a blue *ramie* scarf against her cold neck, not *thwahlja* not
  thwakhijon—
but a subway (*n.*, a long line attaching places, and Frank, they go
  your speed)
ride along line 3 to Insadong with *hanji* finds, black beads and a
  flat red disk
for her neck back home—Frank, that part where her clavicles meet.

*

Annyeonghi gyeseyo meets *čau* at the airport, *n. an unregulated city:*
I'm U.S. before and after Canada, Mexico—Pele, one
  manufacturer of Hawaii,
forbids taking what she makes: I cannot take cobblestones, only
  stones—
curse, *n., v.* (fig.) *return; habitual, patterning movements*
which cannot be exactly duplicated

                              *

the 3-D hexagon toy missing a side rattles in the suitcase, inside,
  mirrors and eyes

a key-chain falls out, too

lumps in the distance clearer and clearer
some say, *nouns*

.... *Preservation/Excavations*

1

The voice box suddenly sang itself, or
the brain grew but didn't grow: "how'd you say... "
... begins a string of shells (beautifully),
or eulogies: life-sized but not realism
bison lowing: reddish and crushed berries
against the first critics: twists of cave rock:
"there's formal and informal... "... hard
to open up or pound out a thing &
still not learn its secret language, & still:
rectangles (gold) and nautilus shells (spires)
make floating & bridges & binaries
crafted numbers: "numbers filament us
into shapes... "... formally introduced as
that. Then.

2

Rain in the morning, they say, always
before more rain. Before cereal,
they remember it's all been eaten:
to say the kitchen door of kitchen
and imply cooking, or the storage
of storage. It is the young wonder
they want back, the dizzy white sparklers
at night, the blue hot fizz of writing
their names in the fog: impractical.
Because old rides in old herds. So they
sing the song of time passing its way
through the hot of hot days, through all the
sentimental doors knobs and door bells:
the usual twists, unusual screws.

3

A spindle of chromosomes grinds up (spoke
& spoken to) until a hard dust floats
in radio up to the stratosphere:
no one sits back in a plastic lawn chair
waiting to say this, no syntax magic
can disappear the problem of letters
describing space then (poof) make more than space
suddenly appear—how osmosis speaks
the continuous flux of the middle
to trick away each beginning, each end,
repetition an anti-vice applied
to the ground and blue-black to make the air
lighter—but words are plastic, and weight seems
able to completely repair itself.

4

It (so it) bubbles to water fountain
fountaining outside the library, froze
for the winter. Blue-white and expanded,
stuck in slow progressive curves, the passing
of edges, knives round and blunted blunter
at little scales, it (it) sits in water—
heat happens to be a small part of it
(in it, the library sits upside down)—
and desires itself away, a way in
to flat points spread out, it-mechanic, it
repairing improvements of its landscape
as landscape: it uses itself inside
itself pronoun after pronoun after
it freezes itself in smaller bubbles.

It freezes itself in smaller bubbles,
it a pronoun after pronoun after
a landscape: it uses itself inside,
repairing improvements of its landscape
in flat points spread out, it-mechanic, it
desiring itself away, a way in,
in it, the library (sits upside down)—
heat happens to be a small part of it
at little scales, it (it) sits in water—
library of edges blunted blunter
stuck in slow progressive curves, and passing
for the winter. Blue-white and expanded,
fountaining outside the library, froze,
it (so it) bubbles to water fountain.

5

Pope said, the one who writes the instructions
writes the thing, that every epic begins

with begging and ends with home, the middle
gets lost, being lost and out of control...

Pope said, your eyes unlock the language key,
text trick and map trap... I'm sorry, Pope said,

I'm only vocals and so far away.
Pope said, if recordings and lies are made

of the same stuff... what's distance, imagined...
I always trusted in circles and spheres.

To throw around seawater is lazy,
Pope said, unless you're also using fire...

...that's metal: the hard, solid thing with flaws,
the fracture hidden under many layers.

6

We have nothing to say. We keep talking:
we, frightened deep thought of cold things machines.
We work patiently away at our lives.

We follow you from hotel to hotel.
Our rendezvous makes us a little less
who we are outside the world outside us.

Our scalpels make dissected animals,
newer and newer layers revealing
sentence structures with wet, frightened letters.

We make a transparent machine, make it
make graphs easy to see through, make it put
important us-things into a number.

We have not forgotten your names, and you
move one move ahead, as calculated.

7

We hurricane and landslide, feel the wave
cheer our feet as we check-point across lines
from continent to continent, your arm
slipping from mine, the question of surprise
too quick to sign or signify the gaps,
nothing present of us left but notes:

Ro

meo

Ro

meo

Jul

iet

Jul

iet

8

The uncle, Cryptozoology,
finds
himself and the aunt buried in gray ruins

and says,
     dig, dig, dig,
to the patient aunt

who loves the uncle very much, and finds him
in places he already is, always
     there there and there, just freshly dug up

so she stands a little off to the side

and watches, here come
          the hullabaloos
pre,
always prehistorically after him,

she says, more the zoology type with
rock-hard scales: feathers: hair: entrails, getting

the blood going, she says, that's sticky, and
uncle digs her
into himself, and is himself

after her, always after her.

9

She says: resonance forgets
what words mean,

first vibration, then a thing, then a ghost,
morphed again,
        naked, reckless with color

the way wind is reckless with air, she says,
the way the earth pushes and folds itself
into explosive wrinkles, volcanoes,

she says all the memory devices
are broken, broken and cannot be fixed,

she says she says she says she says she says:

when I'm asked to be heard, am I hearing
your ear put in the ocean listening
to the floating of fish, like the moon floats,

here,
        she says,
                this wet box of inflections
and reflections in imperfect material.

10

He says, I built this whale from drowned whale bone,
put stained glass windows where the eyes should be,
made the brain from a telescope mirror,
and it sails and sings daily, he says, name
hovering against relief of pages
in darker parts of the dictionary,
he says, the world has grown slick with its oil,
mouths and mouths stuffed with blubber factories
of evolved mentionables evolving
into ears, he says, this quiet kowtow
with the icon, with the light easier
and easier to touch: this is the whale I built
for you, he says, ready-made and intoned
before we ourselves could intone, he says.

11

"It's the way you make me underwater
suspicious. Not just breathablity
but the muffled sound rings traveling out."

& they said the trees were acting squirrelly
&& it was always dusk at the park
&&& the lake never made a noise

I'm writing to remind you, little lark,
not of Dostoyevsky's little stories,
or his little fits, but euphemisms.

"I got every part of everything said
but the last part. How post-post-modernist
blink theory led to post-criticism
of the outer part of the eye. I see."

Then it happened: they sat over bread crumbs.

About the Author

Michael Rerick is the author of the chapbook *X-Ray* (Flying Guillotine Press) and of poems featured in *Fence, Forklift, OH,* and *Tarpaulin Sky*. Originally from Portland, Oregon, he graduated with an MFA from the University of Arizona. While working towards a Ph.D. in English and Comparative Literature at the University of Cincinnati, he won the Academy of American Poets prize. In addition to other awards, he placed in the Summer Literary Seminars (SLS) contest in 2005. He is also a recreational sculptor.

Patricia Carlin, *Quantum Jitters*

Stephen Paul Miller, *Fort Dad*

Harriet Zinnes, *Light Light or the Curvature of the Earth*

Rochelle Ratner, *Ben Casey Days*

Jane Augustine, *A Woman's Guide to Mountain Climbing*

Thomas Fink, *Clarity*

Karin Randolph, *Either She Was*

Norman Finkelstein, *Passing Over*

Sandy McIntosh, *Forty-Nine Guaranteed Ways to Escape Death*

Eileen Tabios, *The Light Sang As It Left Your Eyes*

Claudia Carlson, *The Elephant House*

Steve Fellner, *Blind Date with Cavafy*

Basil King, *77 Beasts: Basil King's Bestiary*

Rochelle Ratner, *Balancing Acts*

Corinne Robins, *Today's Menu*

Mary Mackey, *Breaking the Fever*

Sigman Byrd, *Under the Wanderer's Star*

Edward Foster, *What He Ought To Know*

Sharon Olinka, *The Good City*

Harriet Zinnes, *Whither Nonstopping*

Sandy McIntosh, *The After-Death History of My Mother*

Eileen R. Tabios, *I Take Thee, English, for My Beloved*

Burt Kimmelman, *Somehow*

Stephen Paul Miller, *Skinny Eighth Avenue*

Jacquelyn Pope, *Watermark*

Jane Augustine, *Night Lights*

Thomas Fink, *After Taxes*

Martha King, *Imperfect Fit*

Susan Terris, *Natural Defenses*

Daniel Morris, *Bryce Passage*

Corinne Robins, *One Thousand Years*

Chard deNiord, *Sharp Golden Thorn*

Rochelle Ratner, *House and Home*

Basil King, *Mirage*

Sharon Dolin, *Serious Pink*

Madeline Tiger, *Birds of Sorrow and Joy*

Patricia Carlin, *Original Green*

Stephen Paul Miller, *The Bee Flies in May*

Edward Foster, *Mahrem: Things Men Should Do for Men*

Eileen R. Tabios, *Reproductions of the Empty Flagpole*

Harriet Zinnes, *Drawing on the Wall*

Thomas Fink, *Gossip: A Book of Poems*

Jane Augustine, *Arbor Vitae*

Sandy McIntosh, *Between Earth and Sky*

Burt Kimmelman and Fred Caruso, *The Pond at Cape May Point*

Marsh Hawk Press is a juried collective committed to publishing poetry, especially to poetry with an affinity to the visual arts.

Artistic Advisory Board: Toi Derricotte, Denise Duhamel, Marilyn Hacker, Allan Kornblum, Maria Mazzioti Gillan, Alicia Ostriker, Marie Ponsot, David Shapiro, Nathaniel Tarn, Anne Waldman, and John Yau.

For more information, please go to: http://www.marshhawkpress.org.